Spanish Dancer

Chris Coles

Singapore Art Books
Suite 420, Young Place
Sukhumvit Soi 23
Klongtoey Nua, Wattana
Bangkok, Thailand 10110

www.bangkoknoir.com

Chris Coles
Spanish Dancer/ Chris Coles
ISBN: 9781071303252
1. Spanish Dancer. 2. Chris Coles. 3. Eva Inoue. 4. Geneva. 5. Spanish Dancing. 6. Switzerland

In the summer of 1969, I spent an afternoon at a dance studio in Geneva's Old Town, taking a series of photos of a beautiful woman named Eva Inoue performing a wonderful set of Spanish Dances.

Spanish Dancing is so intense, passionate, proud, full use of the arms, hands and fingers as well as very intricate and loud use of the feet hard against the floor. A powerful dancing style with ancient roots going all the way back to the Spanish Gypsies who had settled in Andalusia and before that all the way back to India.

Total control yet wildly free.

I tried my best to capture the moment.

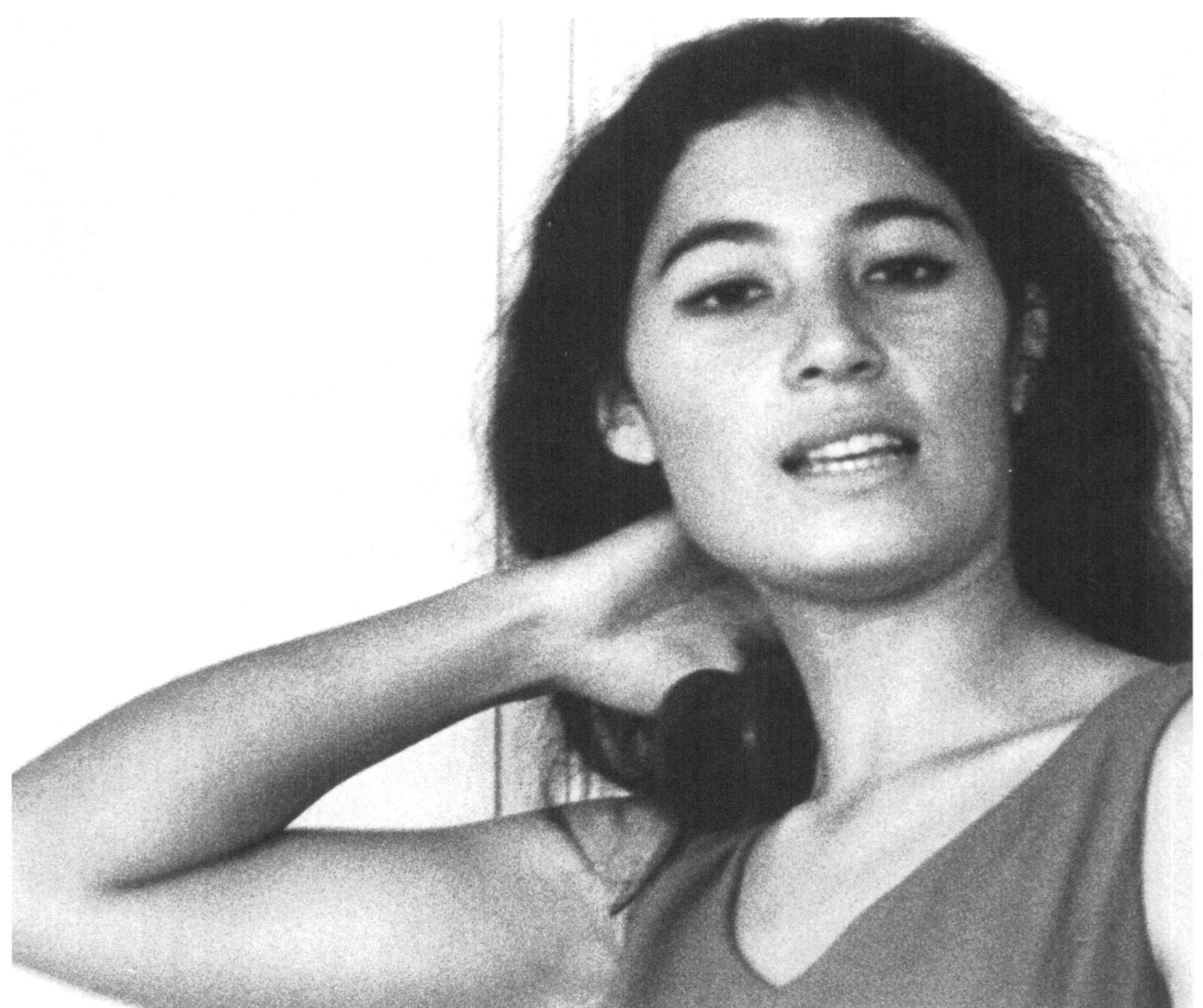

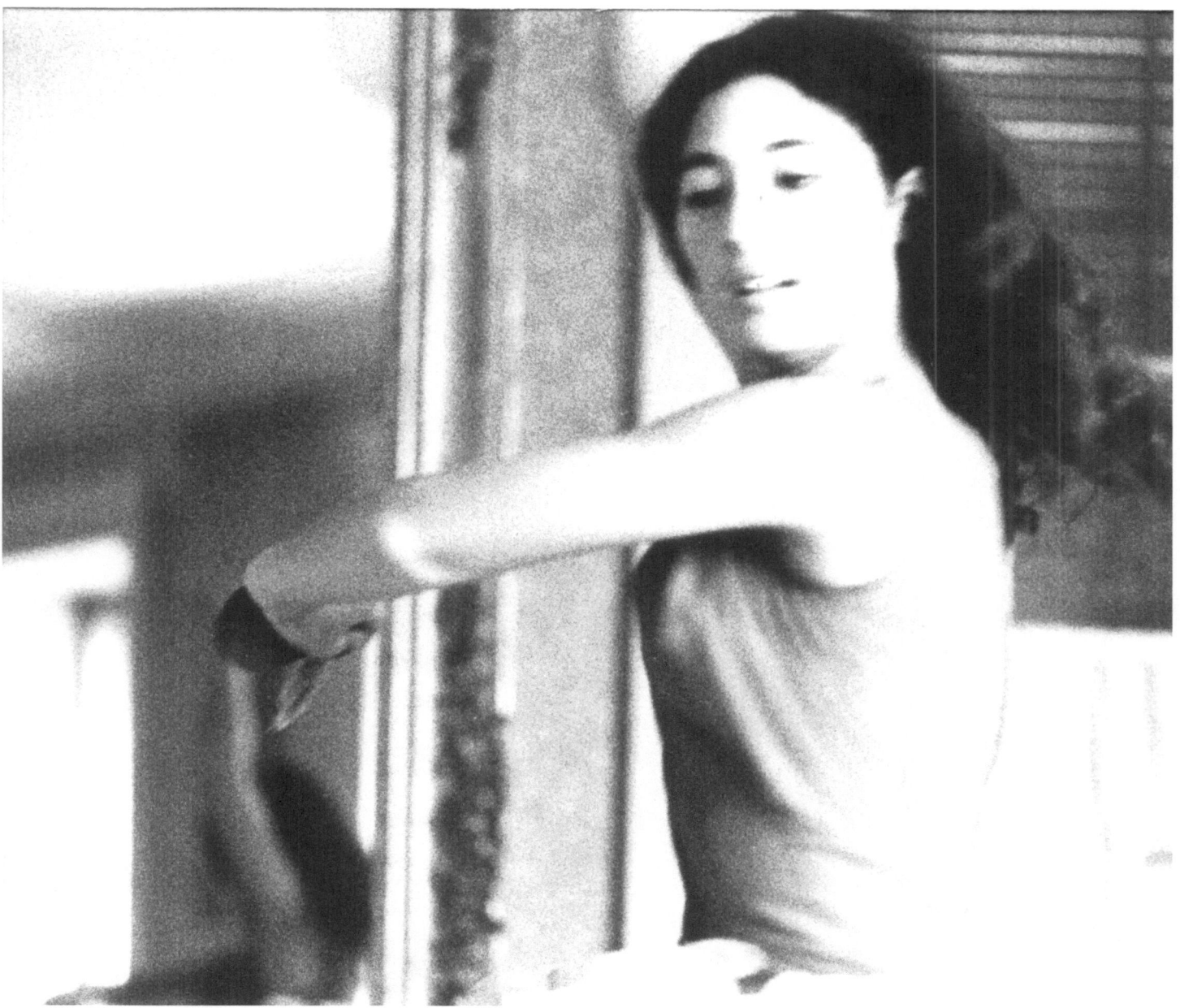

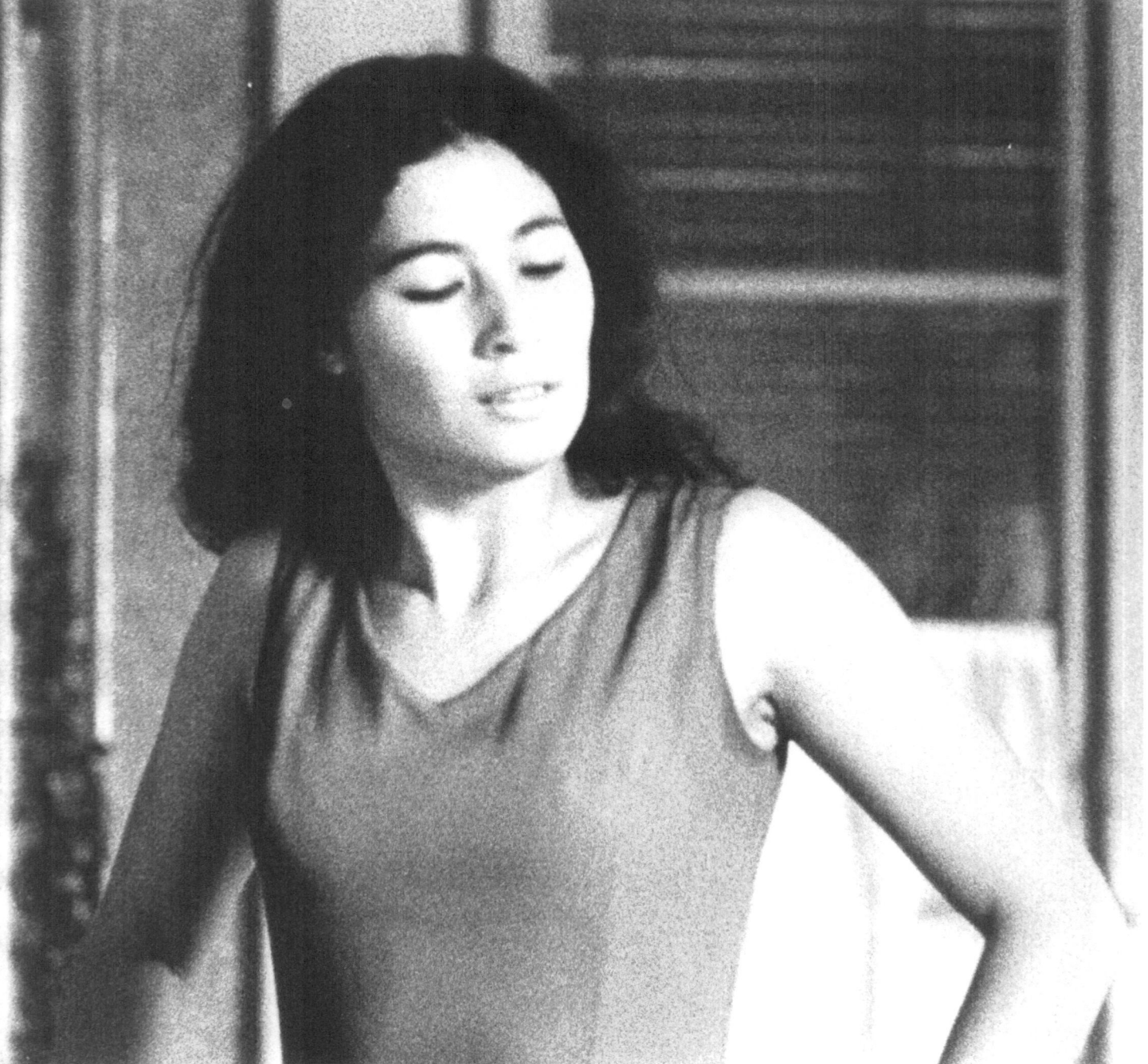

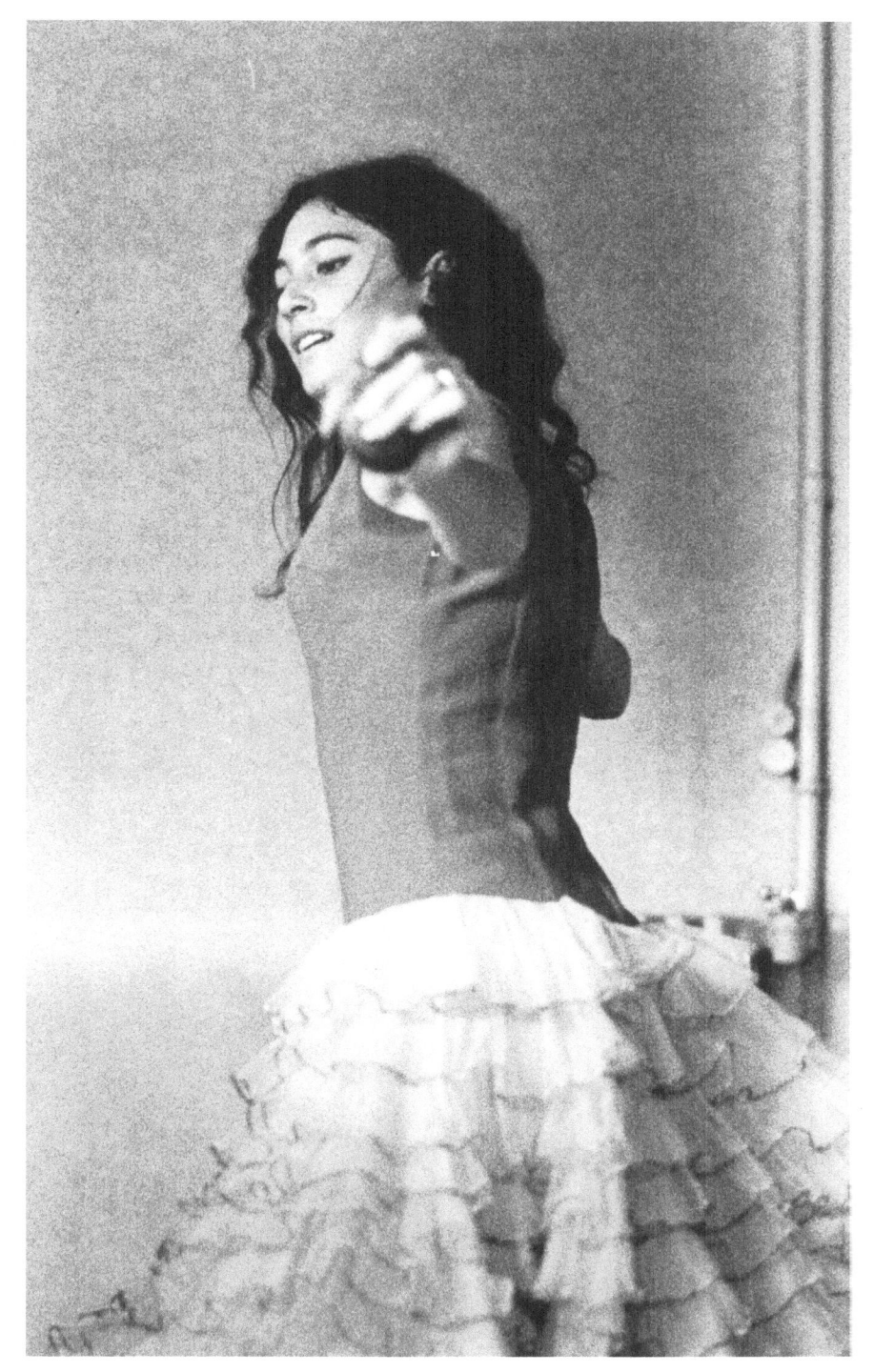

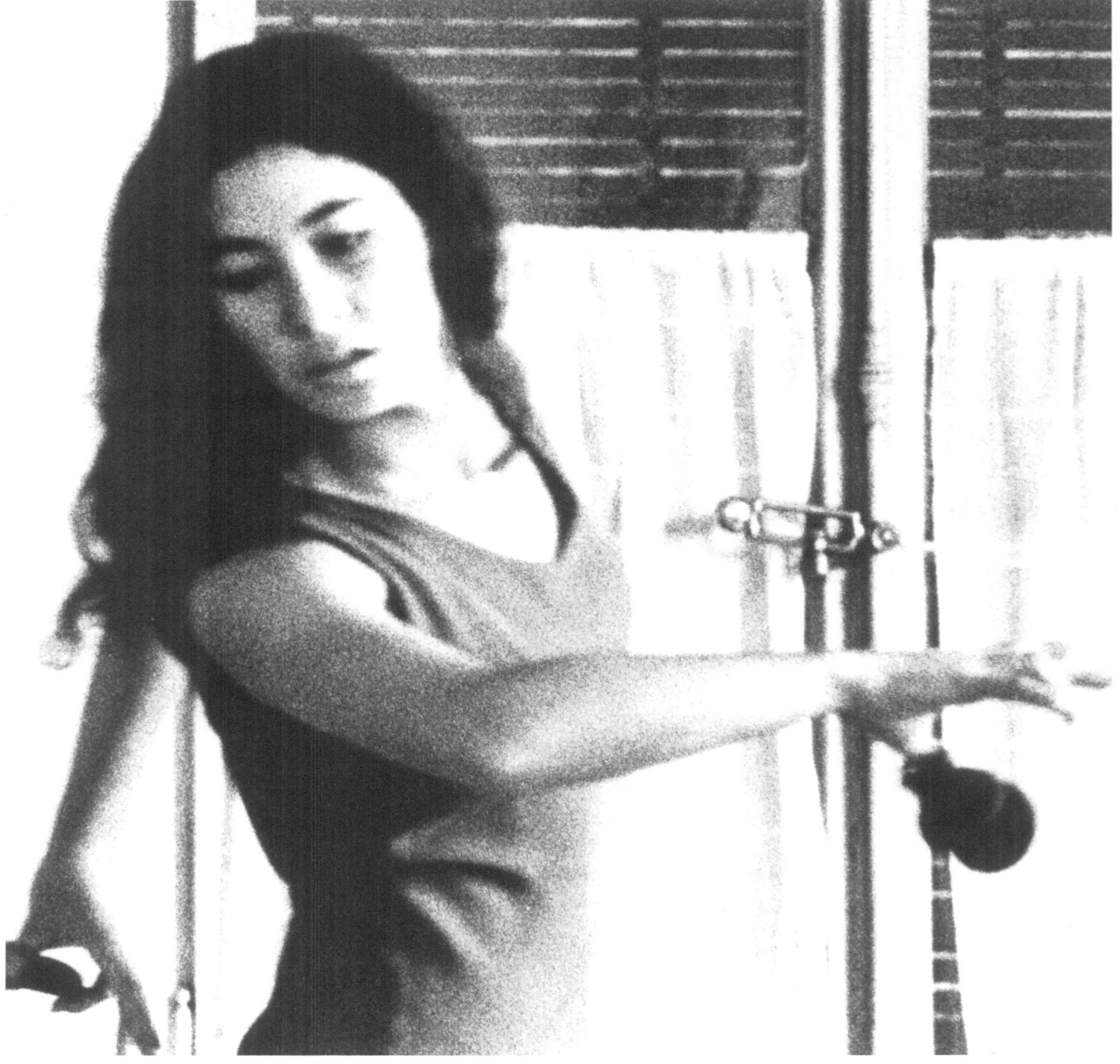

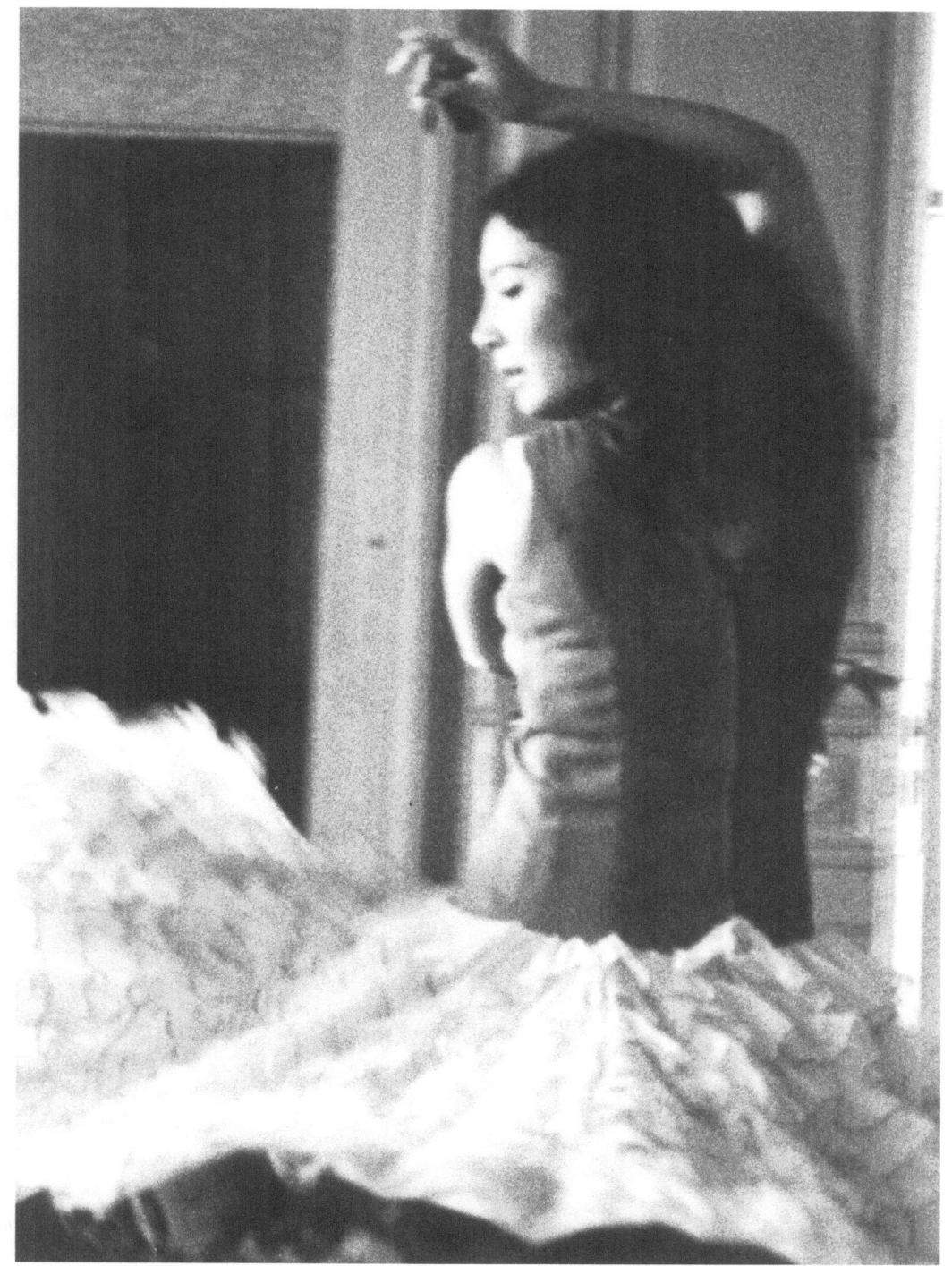

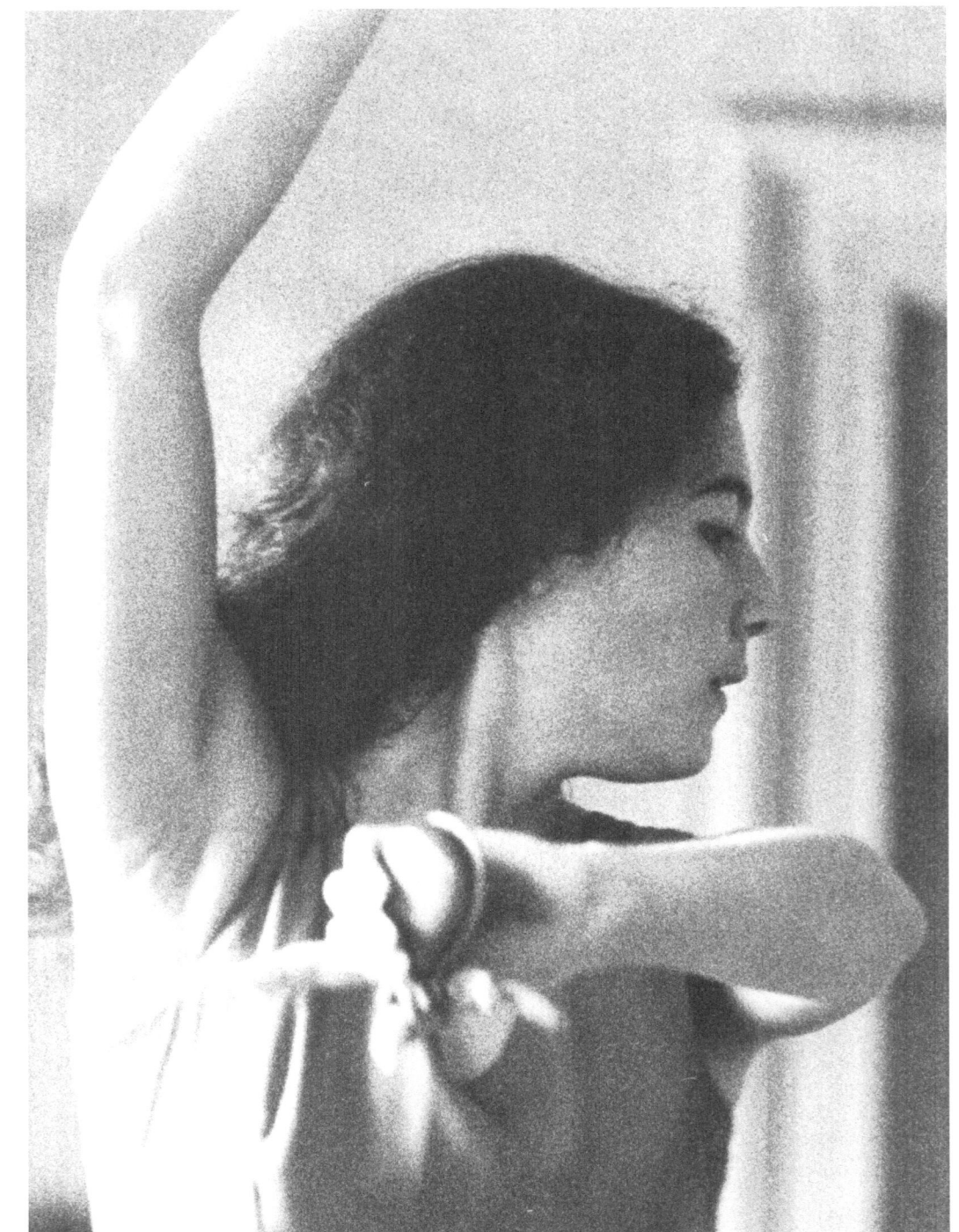

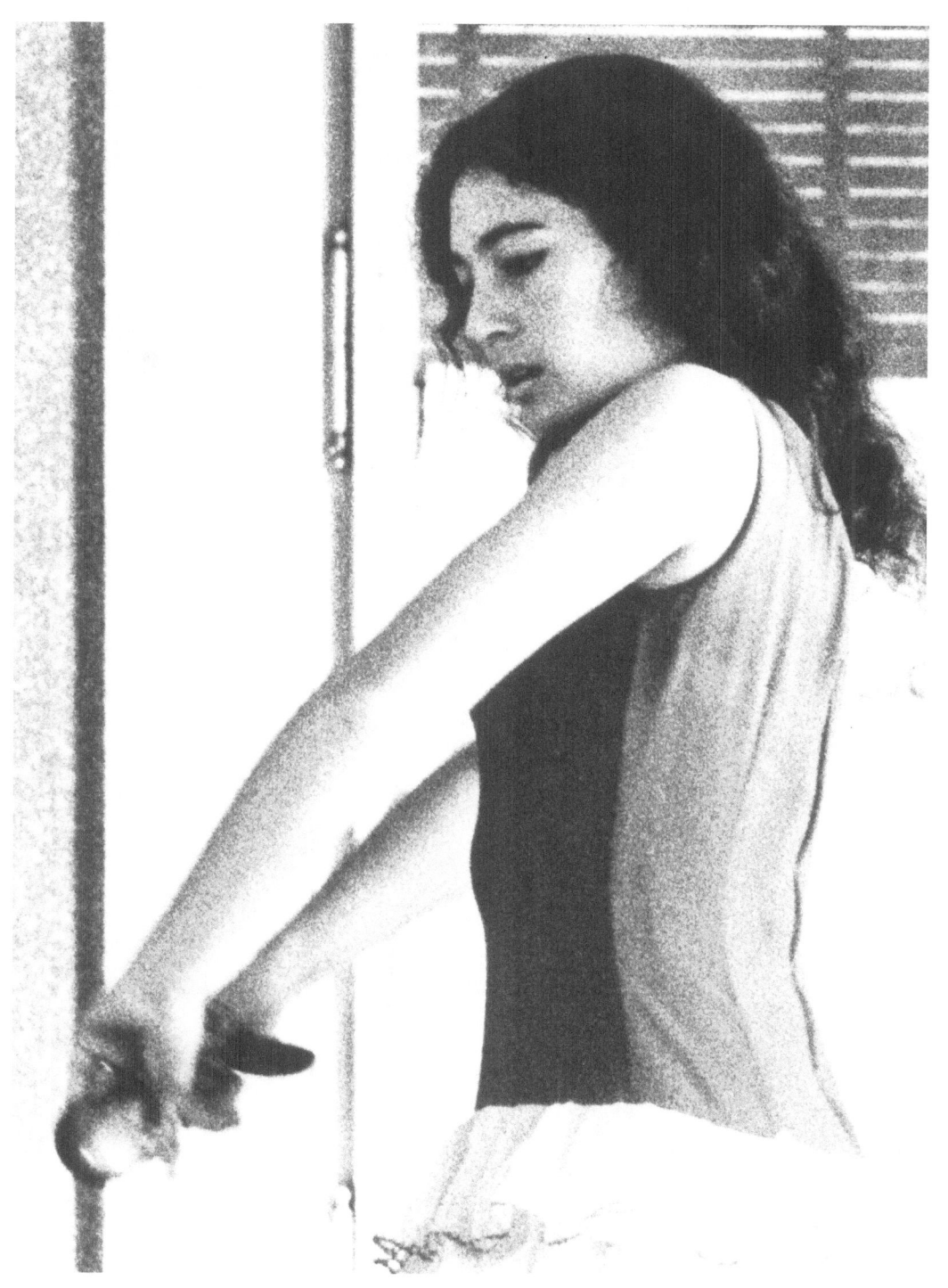

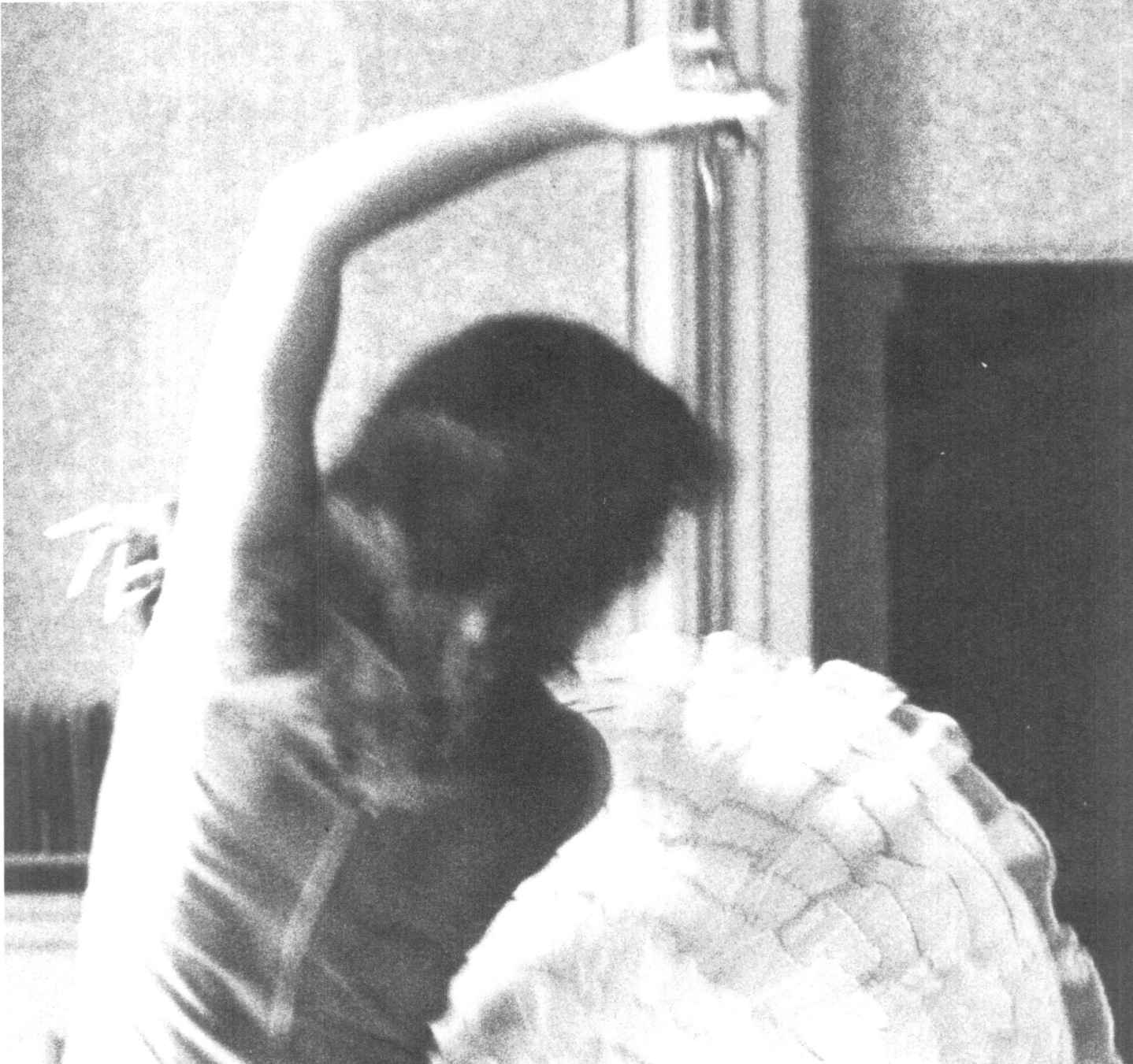

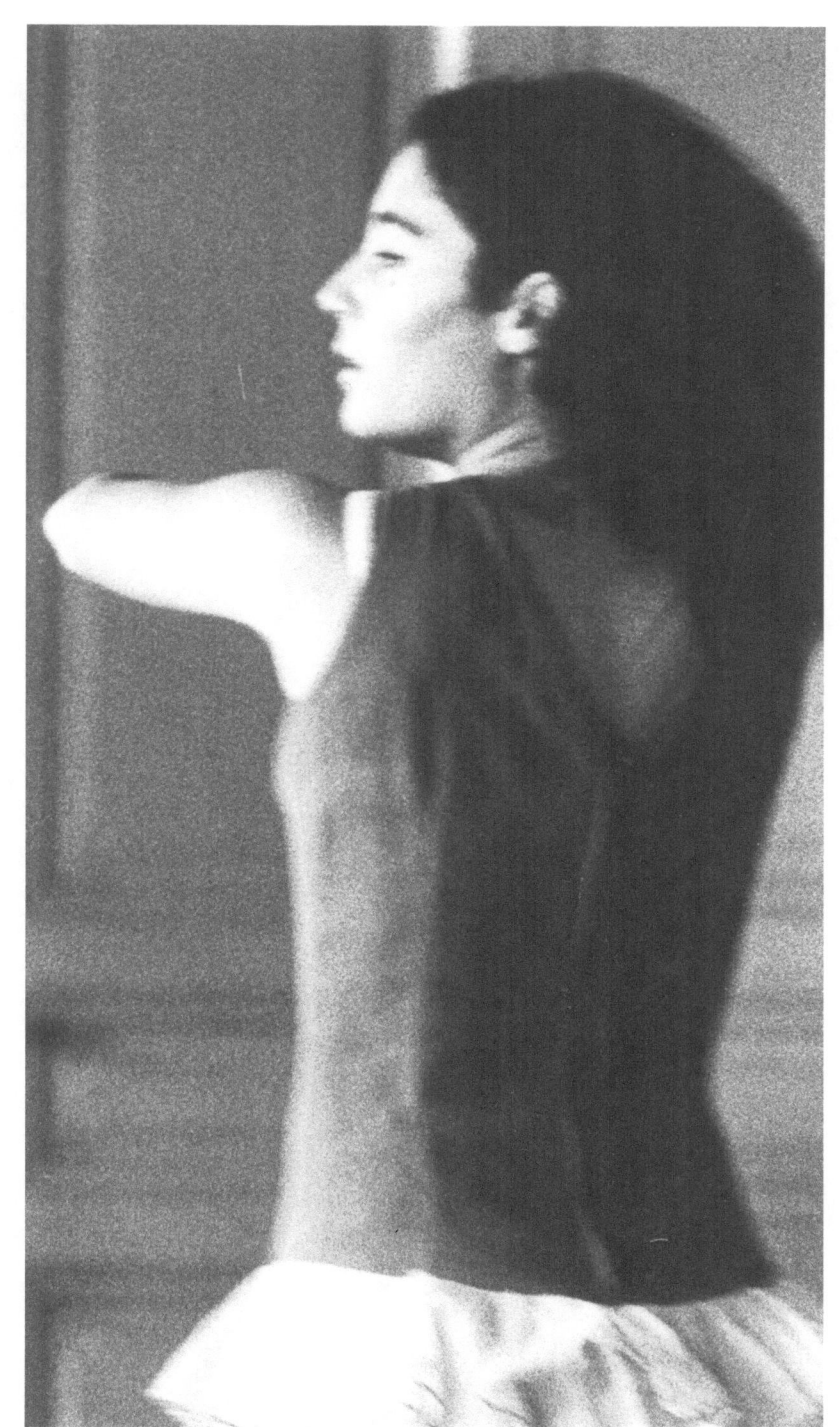

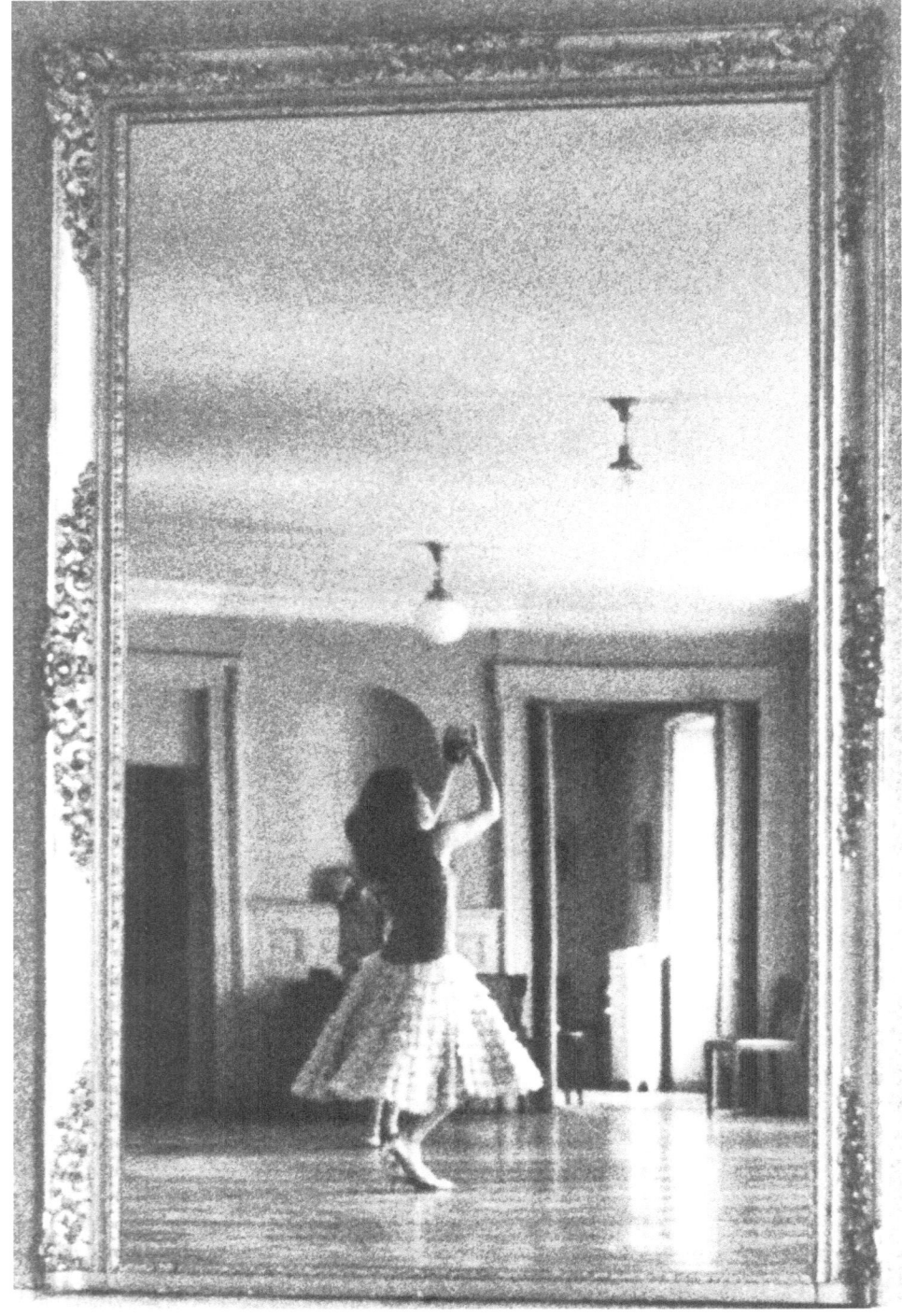

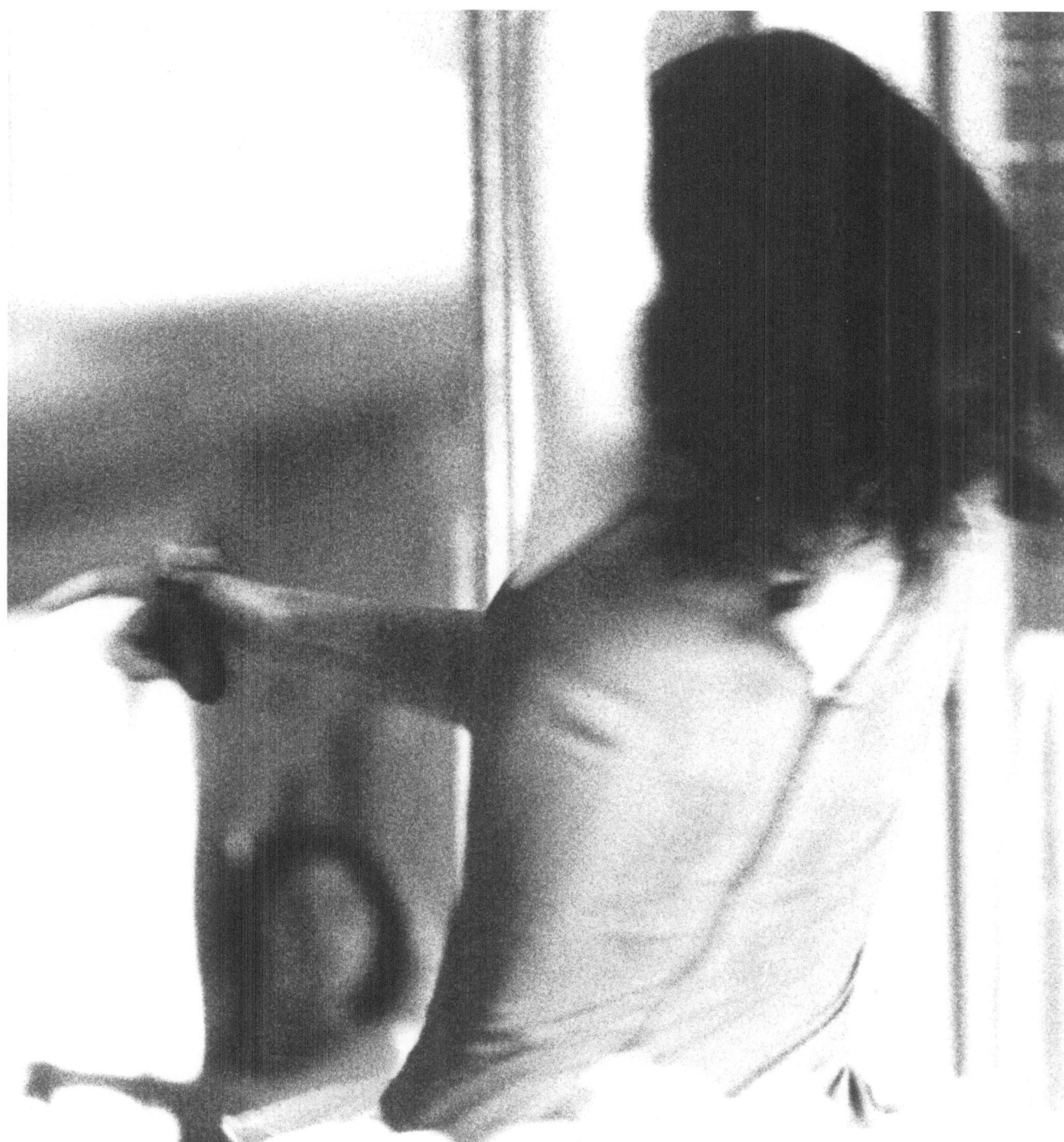

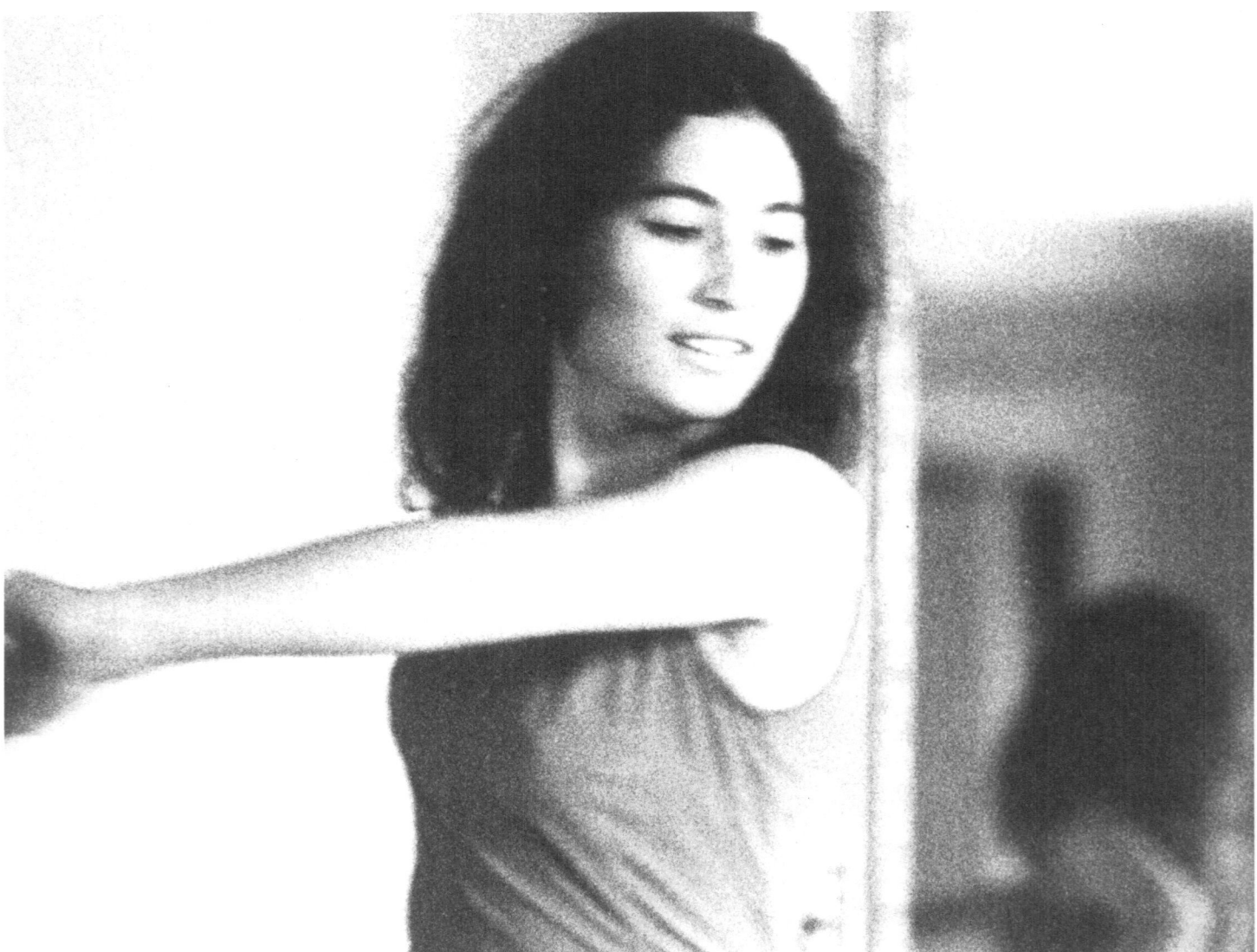

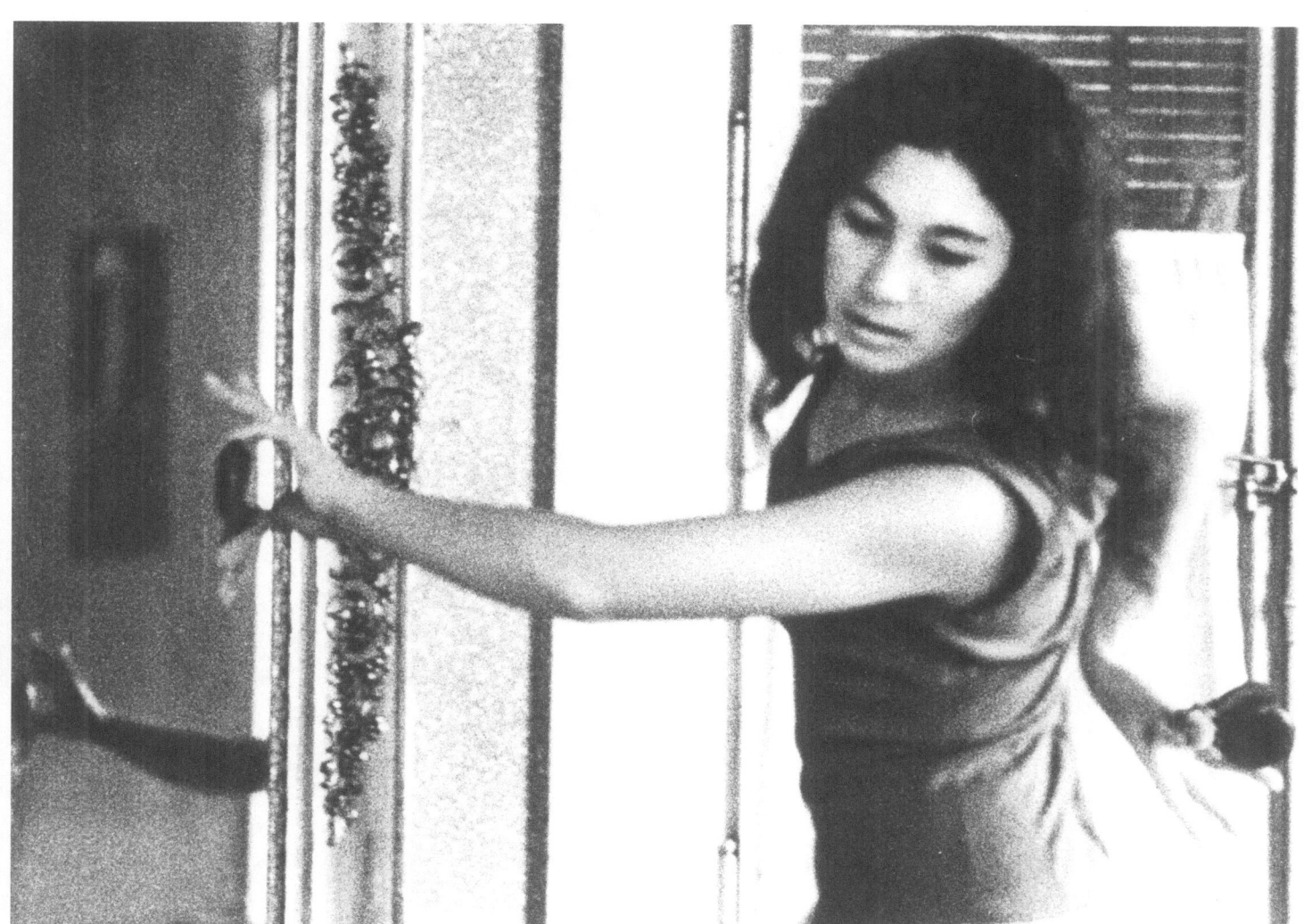

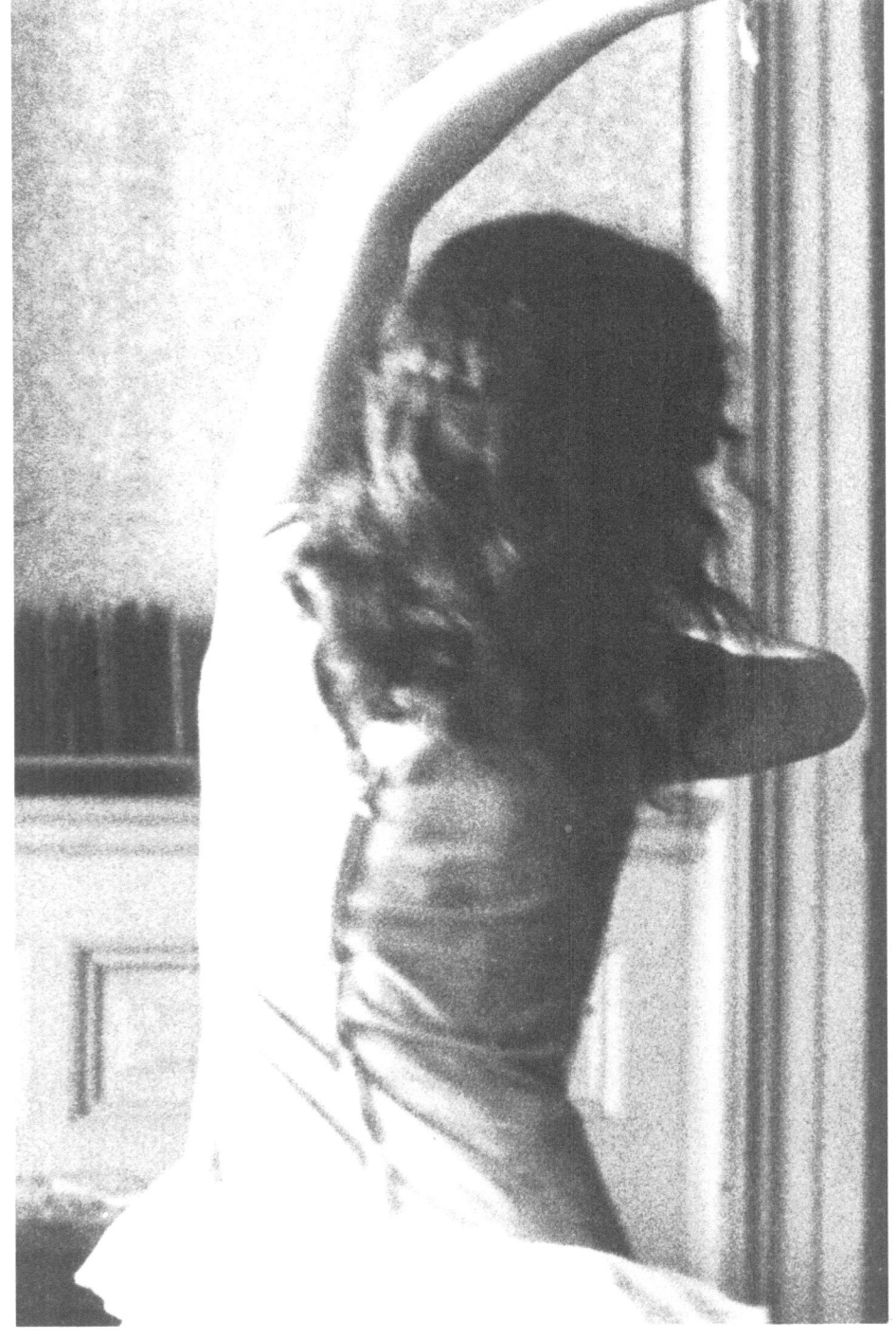

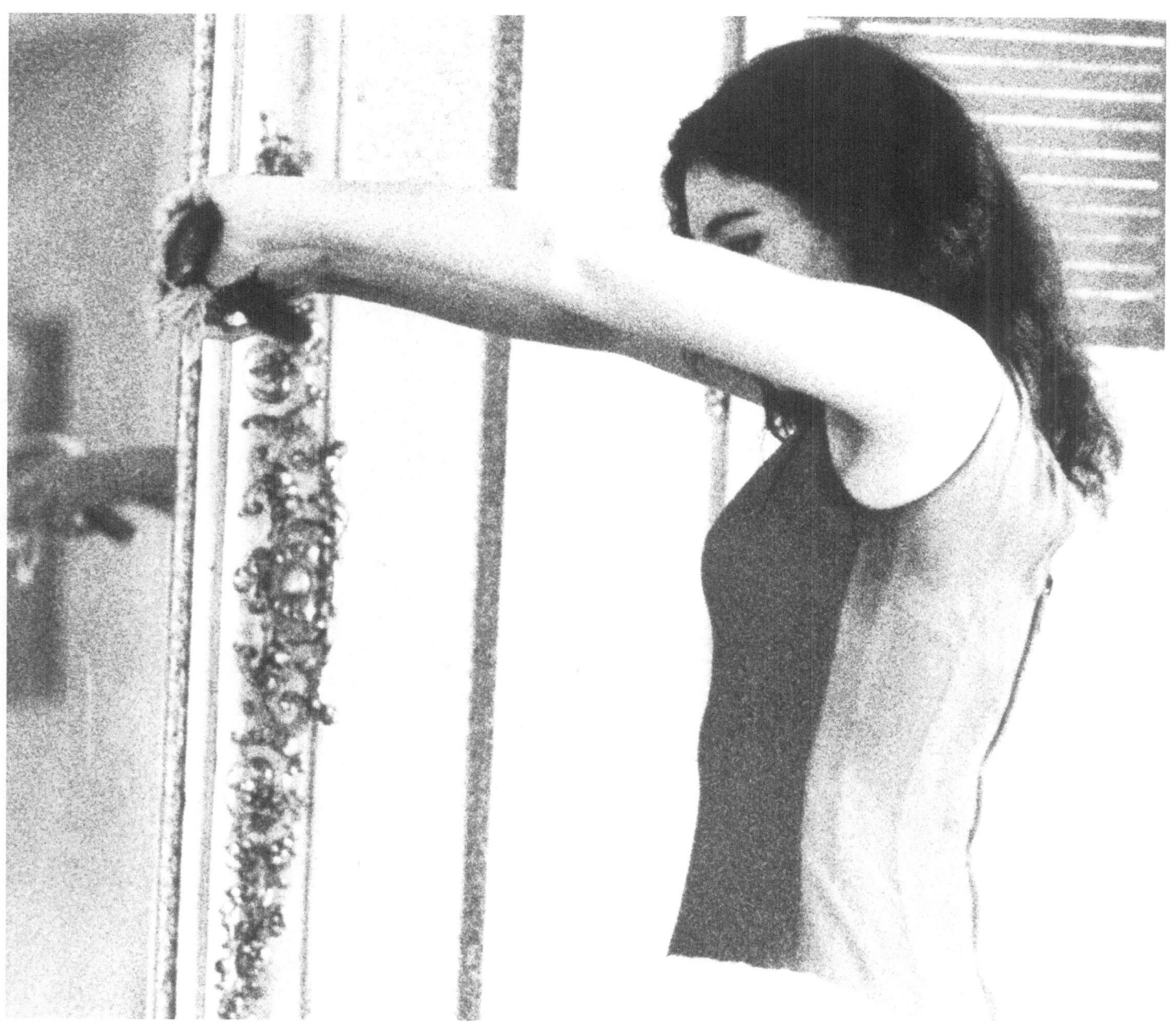

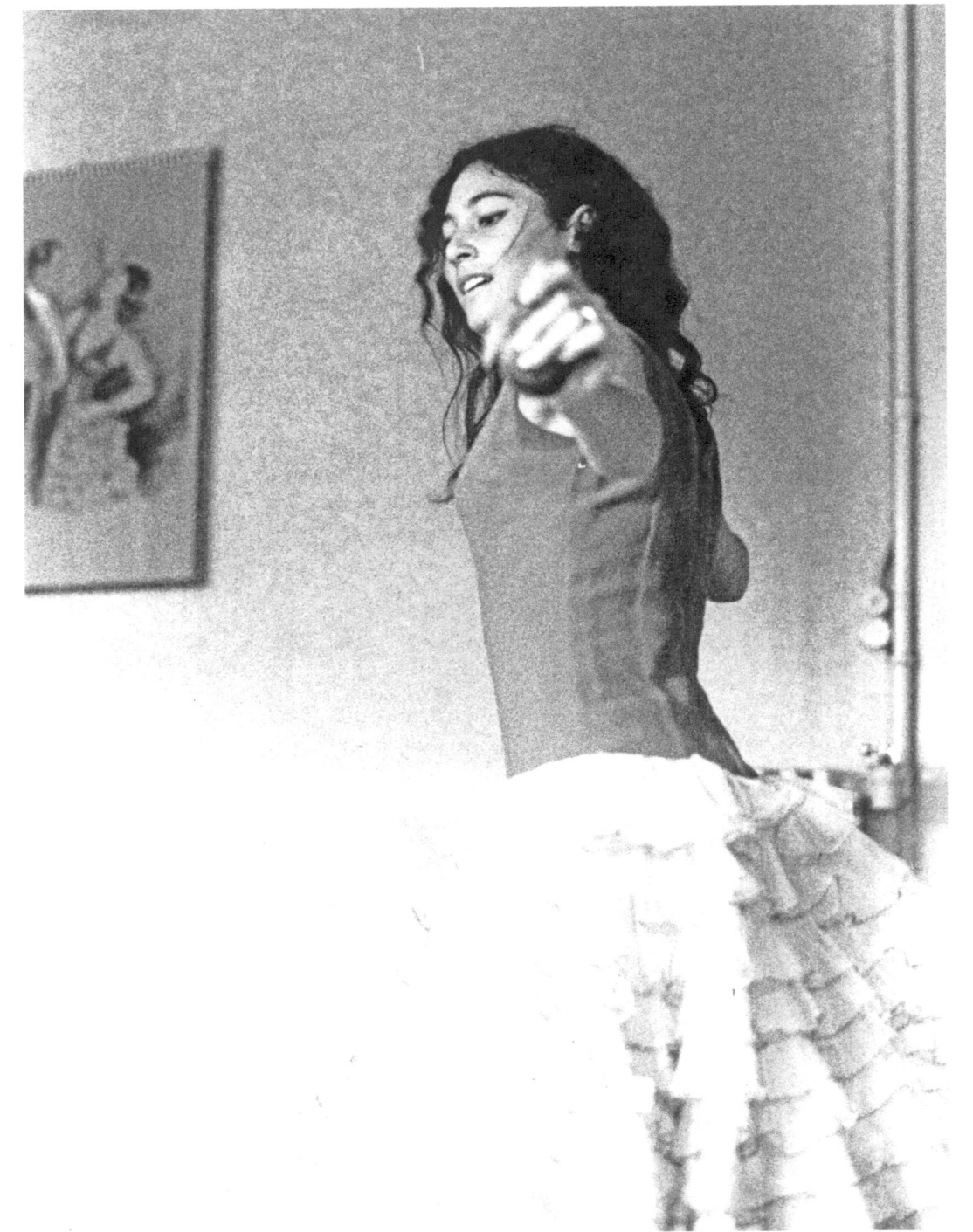

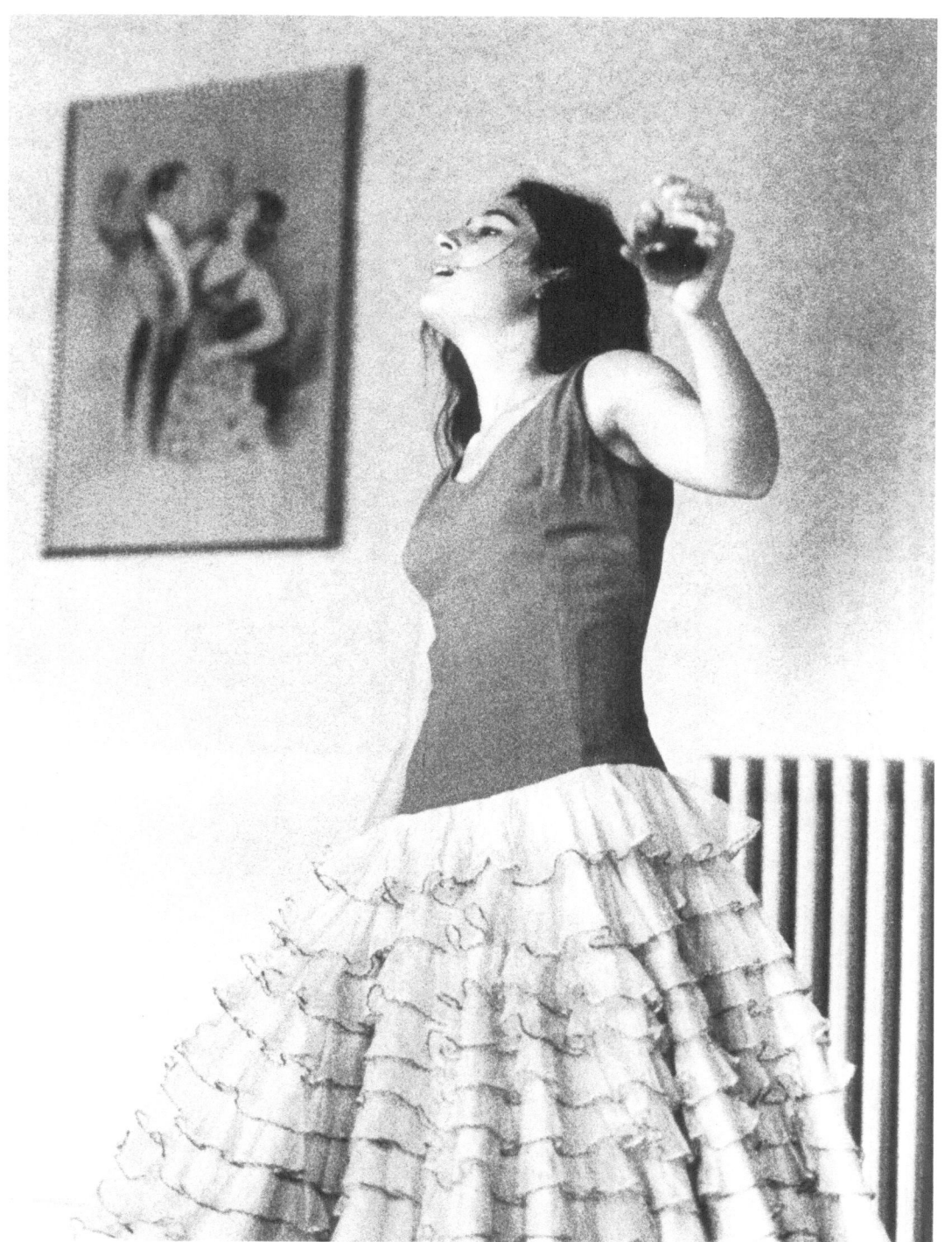

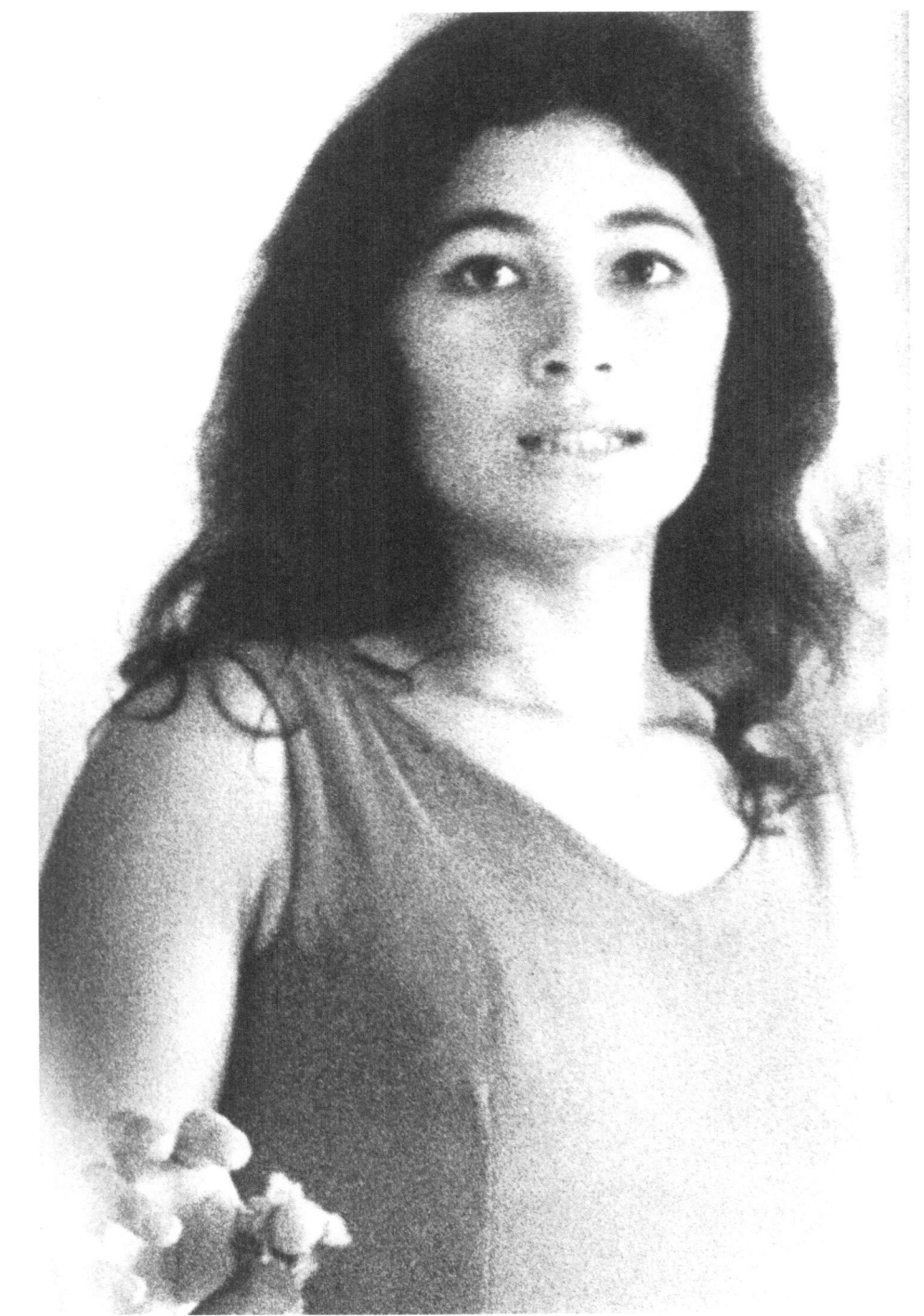

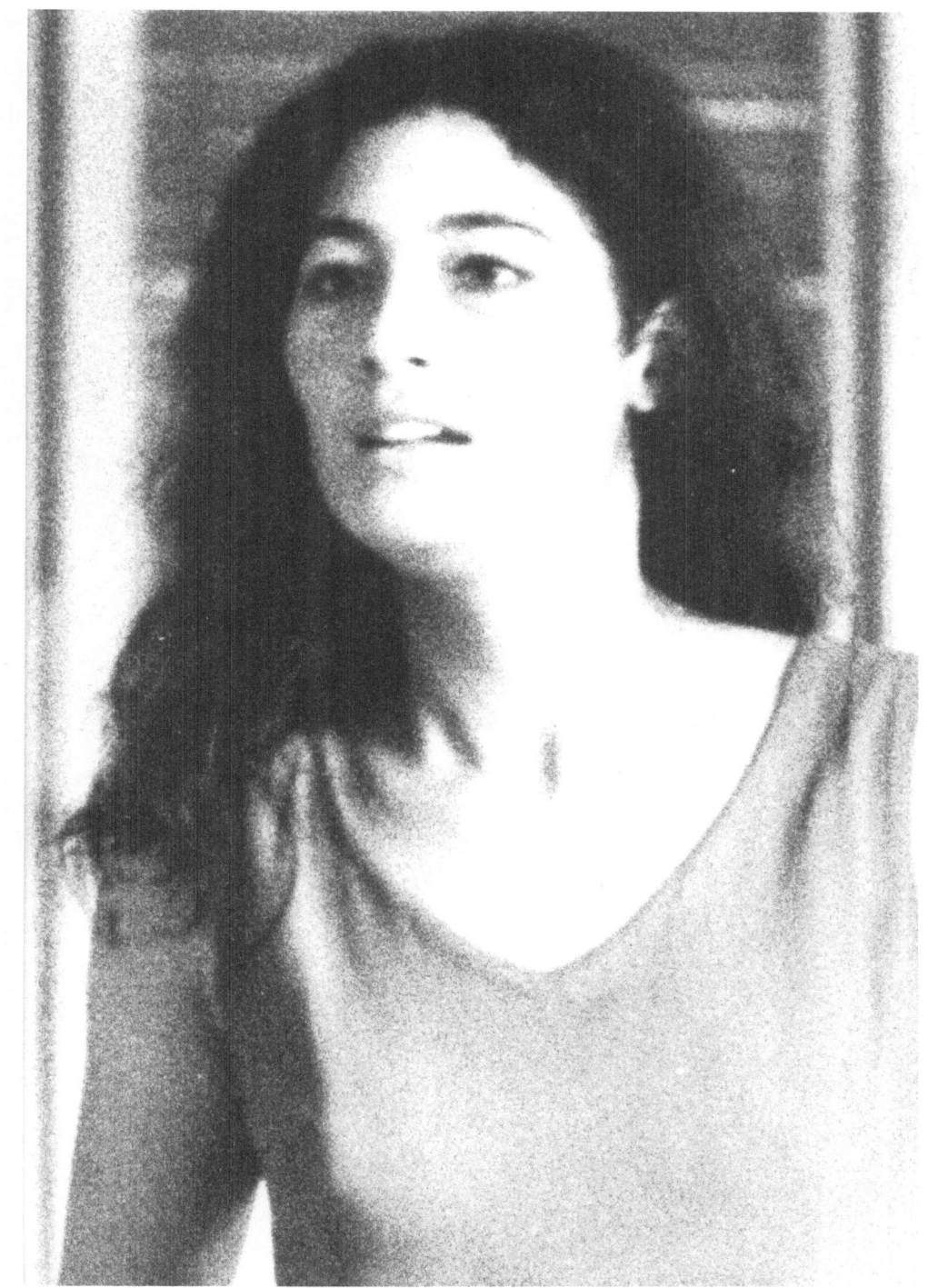

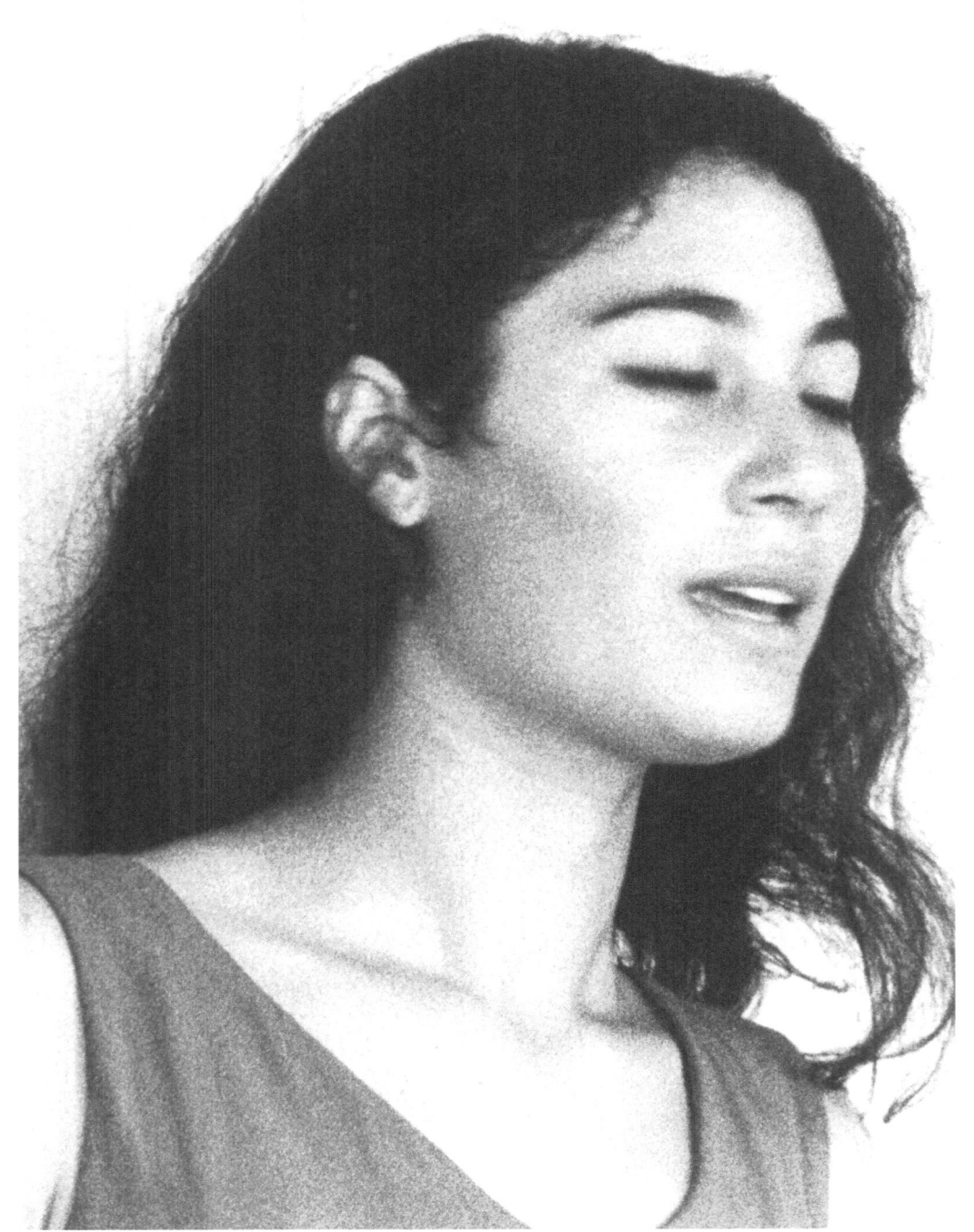

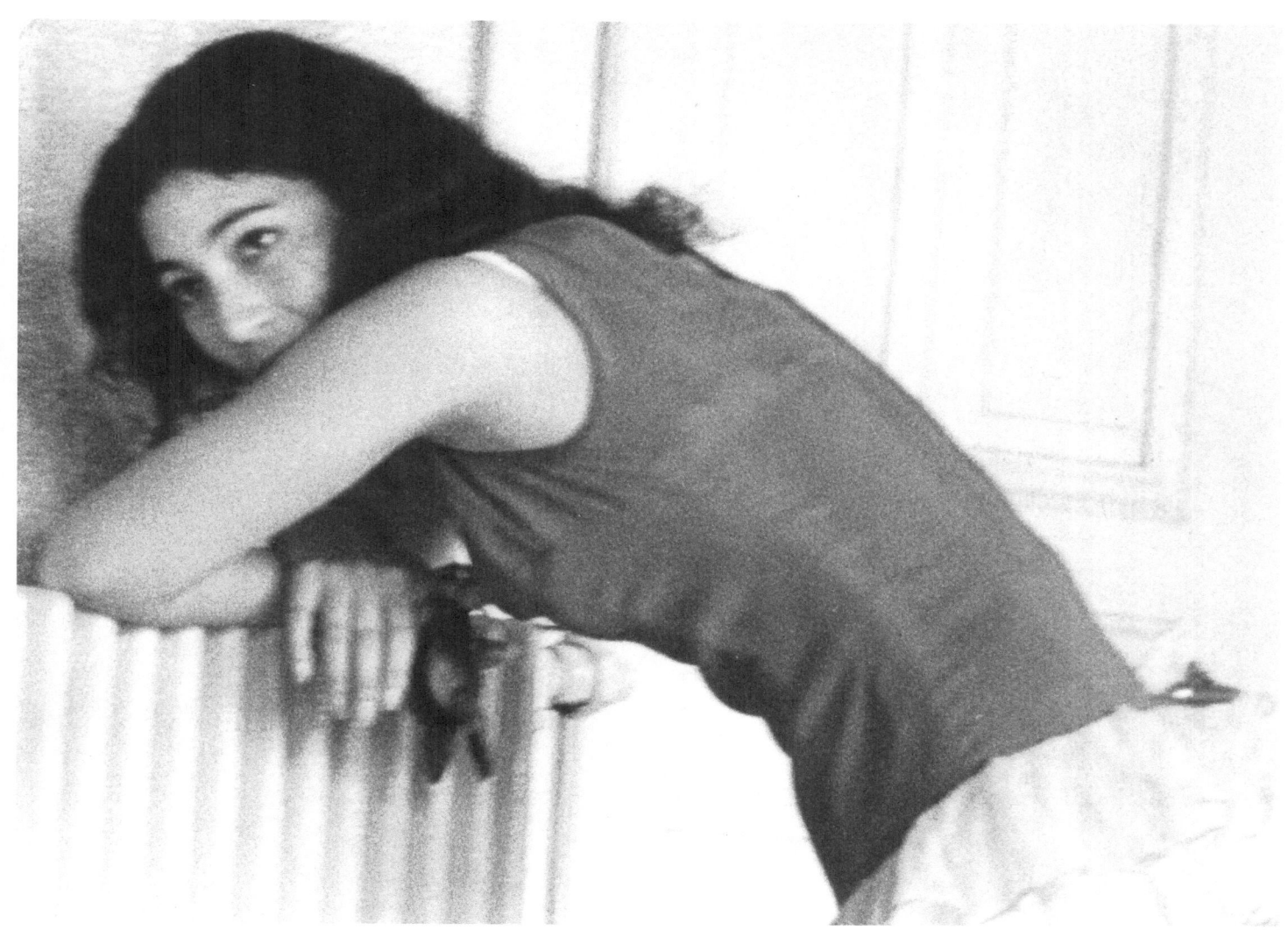

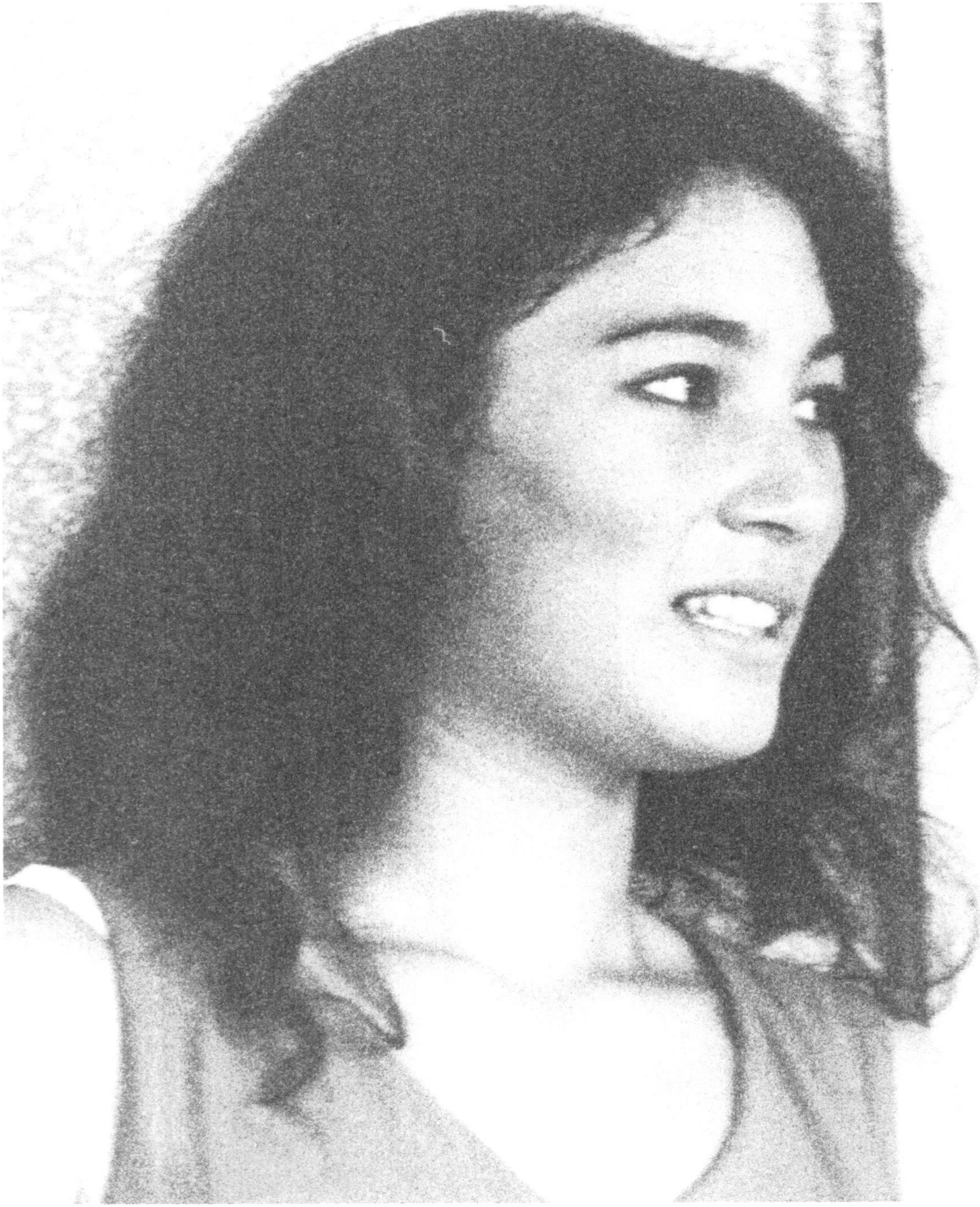

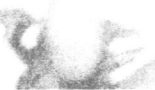

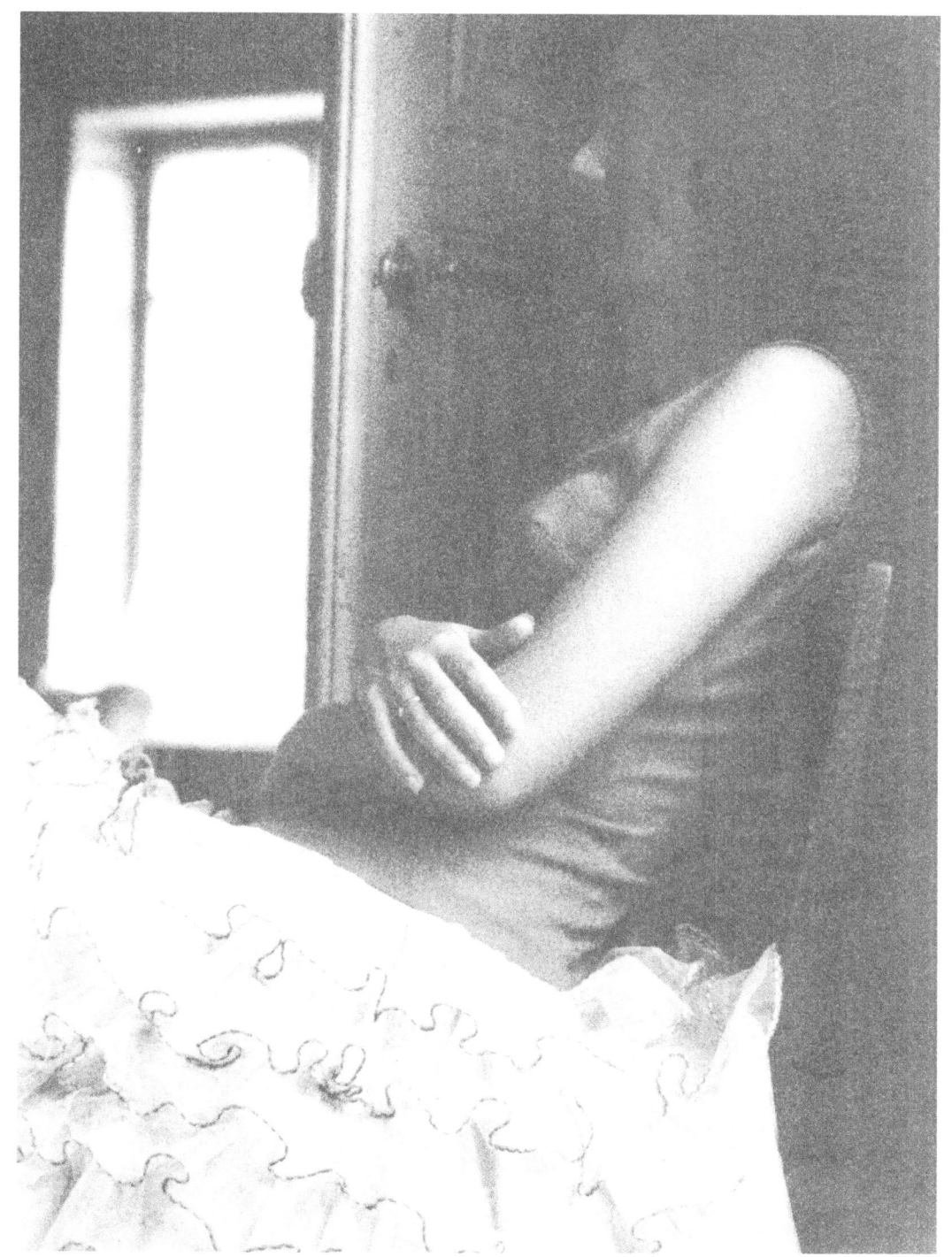

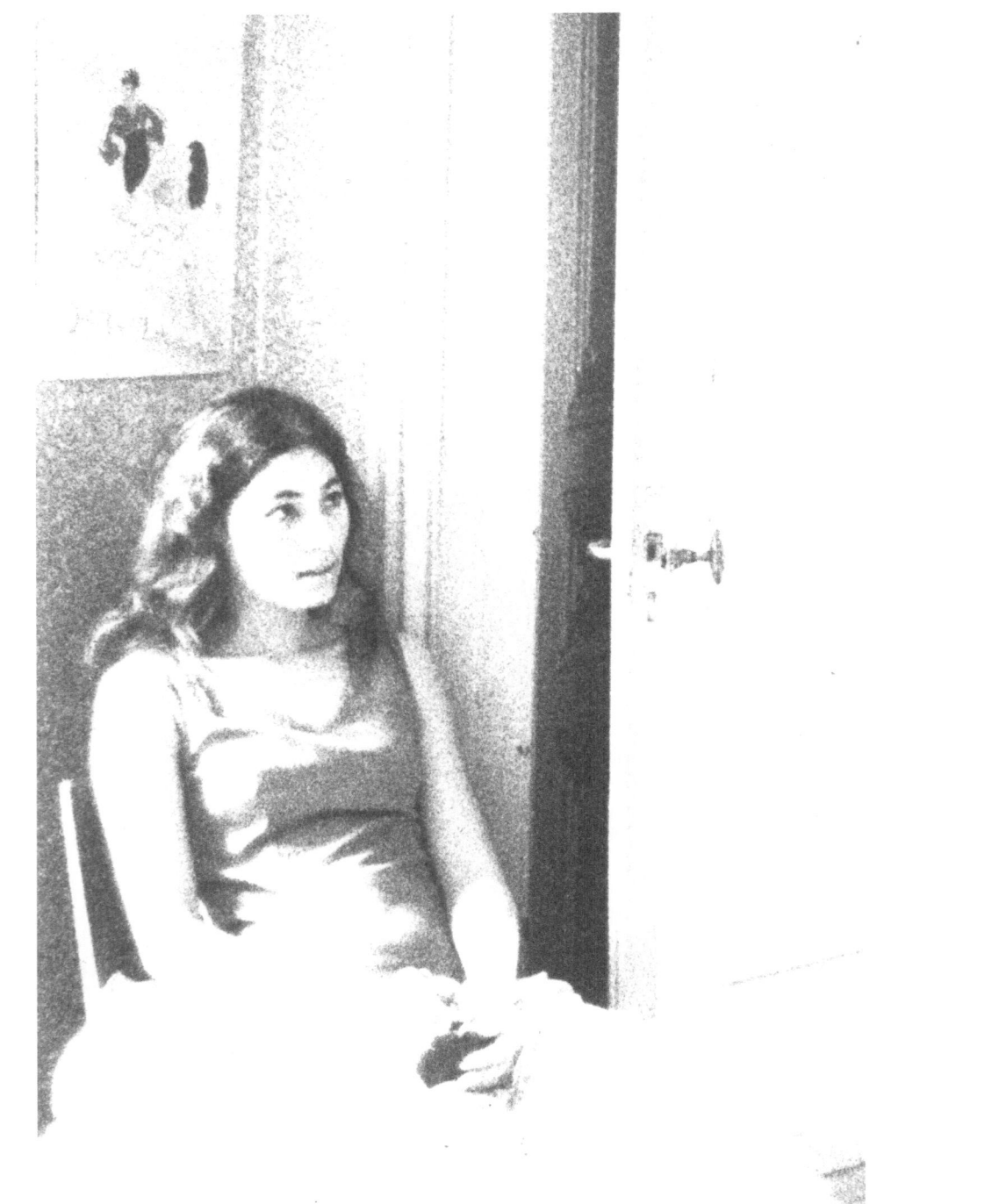

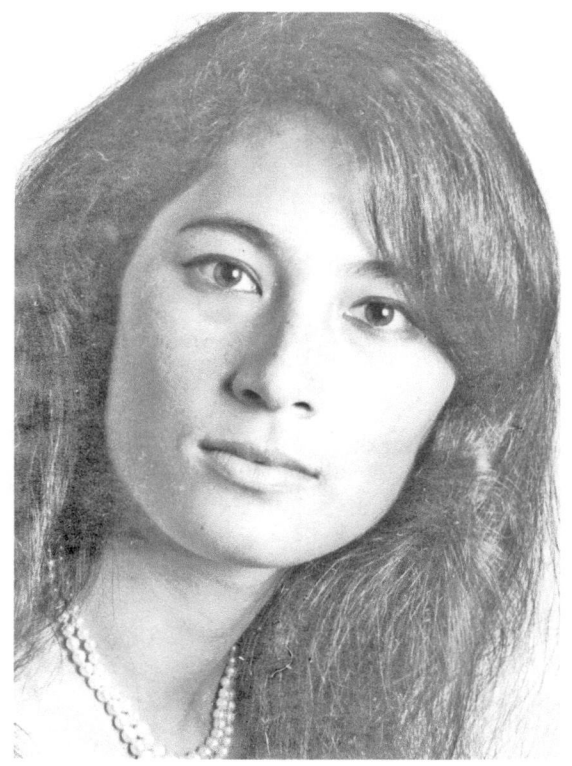

To Eva.........

Chris Coles Books

Bangkok Nights

Navigating the Bangkok Noir

Noir Nights in Phnom Penh

Team Trump Noir

Bangkok Noir in New York

One Night in Bangkok in Singapore

Kris Kolde in the Bangkok Night

Wintertime Santa Monica Beach

Portraits from Bangkok

Patpong Portraits

Bangkok Noir in Pattaya

Colors of the Night

Portraits from the Bangkok Night

German Expressionism and the Bangkok Night

Night Visions

Bangkok Noir at Check Inn 99

Flowers, One Butterfly and the Bangkok Night

Bangkok Neon

Paintings from the Phnom Penh Night

Pattaya Noir